Behind the Scenes

Johanna Rohan

Contents

And... Action!

Going to the movies is fun. The smell of popcorn in the air, the huge movie screen, your favourite actors, the action – how exciting!

Where the Wild Things Are

But how is a movie made? What jobs do people do to get an idea onto the big screen?

Alice in Wonderland

Up

The Producer

The big boss of a movie is the producer. The producer is **involved** at the idea stage, through the filming of the movie, and right up until the movie is ready to be seen.

Jerry Bruckheimer produced *Pirates of the Caribbean: The Curse of the Black Pearl.*

Brian Grazer produced *The Cat in the Hat*.

Producers organise the hundreds of other people that are part of a **movie shoot**. Producers make sure the movie shoot finishes on time, and within the **budget**.

The Screenwriter

A movie must have a story behind it. This is what a screenwriter does – writes a story for a movie!

Andrew Stanton wrote the screenplay for *Wall.E*.

Screenwriters can write many kinds of stories for movies. They can write scary stories, funny stories or sad stories.

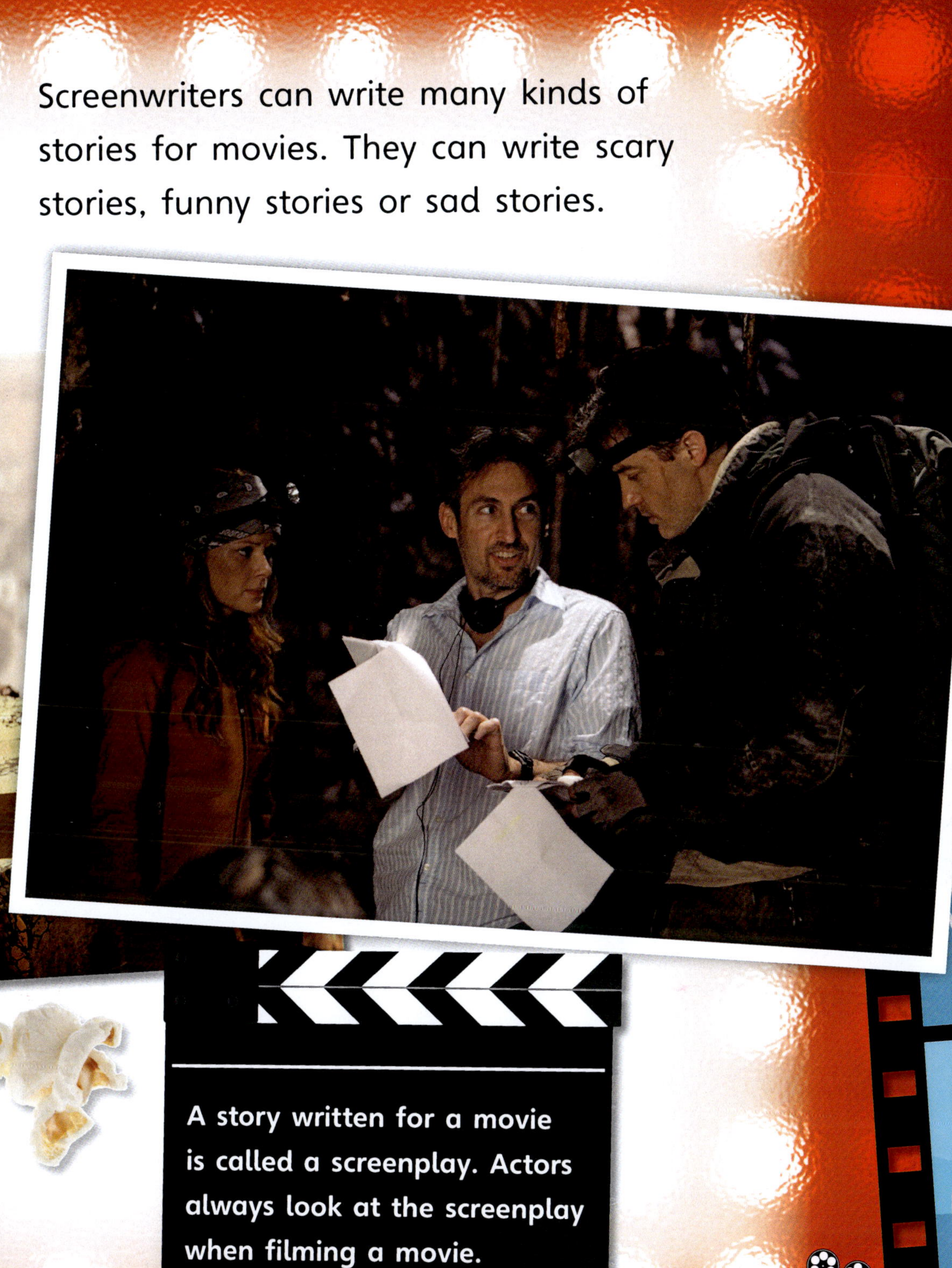

A story written for a movie is called a screenplay. Actors always look at the screenplay when filming a movie.

The Casting Director

Have you ever wondered how your favourite actor became the star of a movie? This is what the casting director does – **hires** the actors.

Casting directors choose which actors will play the different characters in a movie.

Mary Selway was the casting director for *Harry Potter and the Order of the Phoenix*.

Cast List

The list of actors for each **role** in a movie is called a cast list.

Charlie and the Chocolate Factory

Actor	Role
Johnny Depp	Willy Wonka
Freddie Highmore	Charlie Bucket
David Kelly	Grandpa Joe
Helena Bonham Carter	Mrs Bucket
Noah Taylor	Mr Bucket
Missi Pyle	Mrs Beauregarde
James Fox	Mr Salt
Christopher Lee	Dr Wonka

Johnny Depp

Freddie Highmore

David Kelly

The Director

It's the director's job to turn the screenplay into a movie. Directors decide the way the story is told. The director's imagination gives the movie its look and feel.

Steven Spielberg has directed many famous movies, such as *E.T.: the Extra-Terrestrial*. In this photo from 1982, he is directing the lead actor.

Spike Jonze directed *Where the Wild Things Are*.

George Lucas directed *Star Wars II: Attack of the Clones*.

The director gives orders, or directions, to everyone working on a movie.

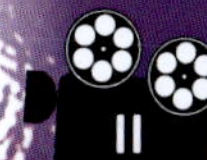

The director:

- gets the movie ready to be filmed. This is called pre-production.
- shoots the movie on film. This is called production.
- puts the movie together. This is called post-production.

George Miller directed *Happy Feet*.

Directors can make a movie look any way they want. One way they do this is with camera angles. Filming an actor from far away gives a different feel than filming the actor close up. See?

The Storyboard

The storyboard is the story of the movie, drawn in pictures. Every **scene** in the movie is drawn!

Storyboard: *Aliens on Holiday*

Shot 1: the beach.

Shot 2: the spaceship landing.

Shot 3: aliens leaving their spaceship.

Shot 4: an alien looking at the beach.

Before a movie begins filming, the director plans it on paper. When filming begins, the director knows exactly what to do!

Shot 5: the alien's face.

Shot 6: aliens walking along the beach.

Shot 7: aliens setting up a beach spot.

Shot 8: aliens relaxing!

The Production Designer

The production designer's job is to make sure the **movie sets** are just how the director wants them. The production designer also makes sure that the movie's "look" is right for the time in which the movie is set.

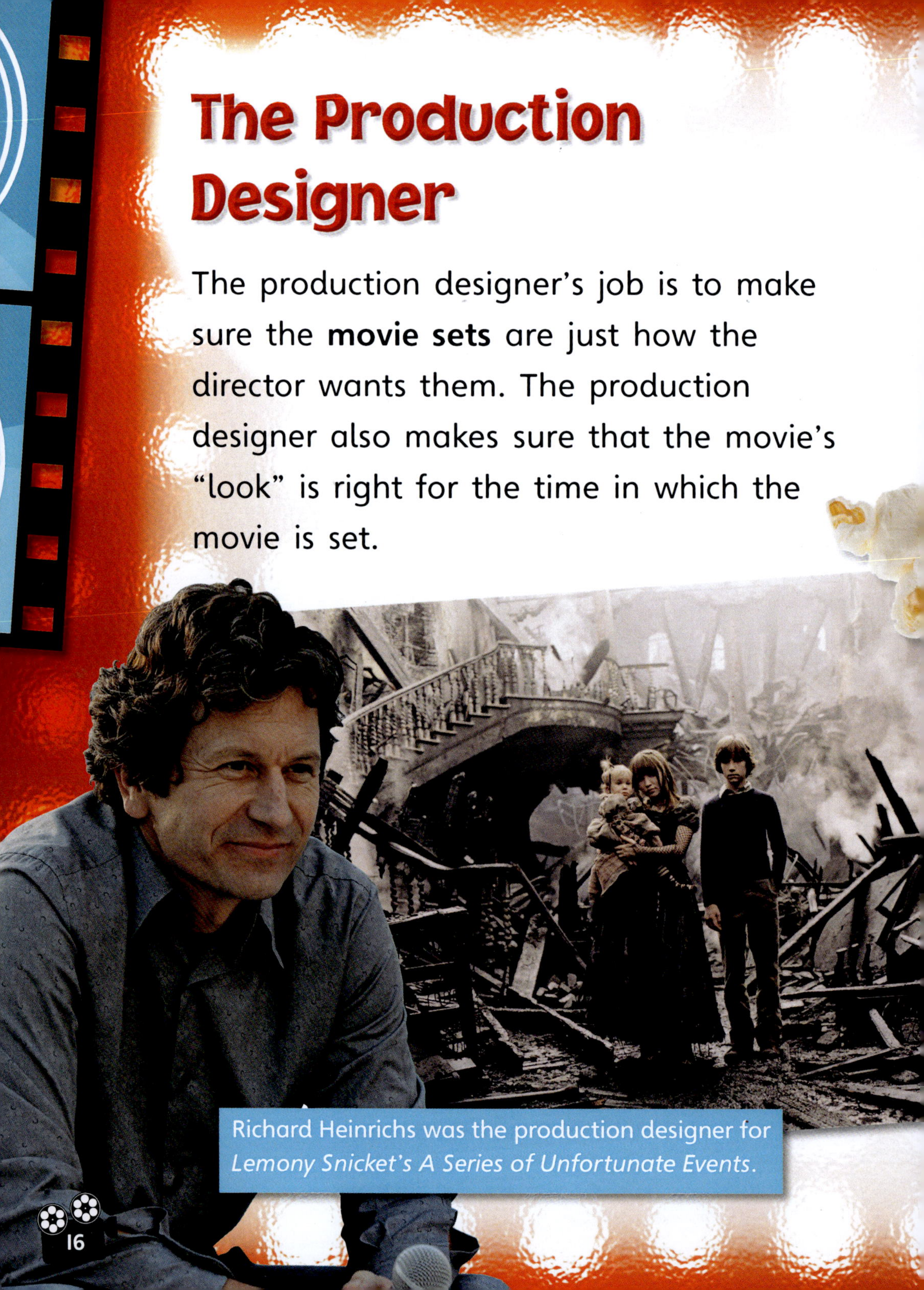

Richard Heinrichs was the production designer for *Lemony Snicket's A Series of Unfortunate Events.*

Production designers are in charge of many people working on a movie set. These include the costume designers, set designers, special effects people, make-up artists and many more. Phew!

Night at the Museum: Battle of the Smithsonian

The Cinematographer

The cinematographer's job is to get the right images on film that best tell the story. They take the director's ideas and set up the camera shots.

Cinematographer Bruno Delbonnel at work on the set of a Harry Potter film.

A cinematographer is also called the "director of photography".

The cinematographer is also in charge of:

- the lighting
- the camera lenses
- the film that the movie is shot on.

The Make-up Artist

The make-up artist's job is to make the actor look like their character. The character could look normal – just like you or me – or the character could look really weird and scary!

The make-up artist works on an actor's face, hair and body using special make-up skills.

Eddie Murphy

They can make someone look older or younger, pretty or ugly, or even monstrous!

Ralph Fiennes

Extras

Extras are people who have non-speaking roles in movies. Extras appear in the background of movies, such as in crowd scenes. Some movies have hundreds, even thousands of extras!

A crowd scene from *Lord of the Rings: The Two Towers.*

Everyone Has to Start Somewhere!

Did you know the famous actor Brad Pitt started out as an extra? Shirley Temple was also an extra before she became one of the most famous child stars of all time!

Shirley!

Brad!

An extra is also called a "background actor".

Stunt Doubles

Many **movie stunts** are too dangerous for actors to do themselves. Enter the stunt double! The stunt double takes the place of the actor when dangerous and crazy stunts are needed.

A stunt being filmed for *Spiderman 3*.

A martial art stunt in *The Mummy: Tomb of the Dragon Emperor.*

To kick-start your stunt career you must get fit, healthy and skilled!

Learn:

- gymnastics
- swimming
- horse riding
- rock climbing
- snow skiing
- martial arts – *hii-yaaa*!

Stunt doubles are sometimes called "stunties"!

The Editor

The editor turns the hundreds of hours of film, shot by the director, into a movie around two hours long. The editor takes out the bad bits, and puts together the good bits to make the final movie.

Editor Andrew Adamson edited the movie *The Chronicles of Narnia: Prince Caspian*.

When you watch a movie, it seems like everything was shot in order. All the sounds and images work together perfectly – that is the magic of film editing!

You're Called What?!

As a movie's **credits** roll, have you ever read some of the strange jobs listed?

Gaffer

The gaffer is the head of the **electrical** department. The gaffer is in charge of the lighting for a movie.

Key Grip

The key grip is the head of the set department. The key grip is in charge of the **carpentry** of a set.

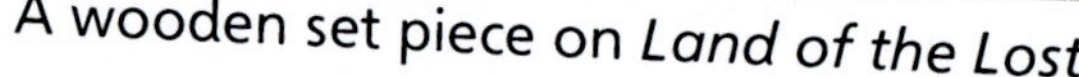
A wooden set piece on *Land of the Lost*.

Best Boy

The best boy electrical helps the gaffer. The best boy grip helps the key grip.

Clapper

The clapper is the person with the clapper board. The clapper "claps" it shut in front of the camera.

Film Speak

If you want to work in movies, you'll need to know what people are talking about on set.

"Action!"

The director shouts "Action!" when the actors need to begin performing.

Close-up

A close-up is when an actor's face fills up most of the screen.

"Cut!"

The director shouts "Cut!" to stop the actors performing.

Take

A take is a scene that has been filmed, or is being filmed.

"That's a Wrap!"

This means that filming is over for the day, or over for the whole movie!

Guess what? You have finished this book, so... **That's A Wrap!**

Glossary

budget an amount of money set aside to pay for something

carpentry things that are built from wood

credits a list of the people who worked on a movie

electrical having to do with electricity

hires gives someone a job

involved is part of

movie sets the different scenery for a movie

movie shoot the filming of a movie

movie stunts actions to be performed in a movie, often dangerous

role the part played by an actor

scene a part of a story

Index